DISNEY
LEARN TO DRAW
MICKEY and MINNIE

Illustrated by
Todd Kurosawa
Pattie Tomsicek
Diana Wakeman

Walter Foster

Hi, Friends!

You are going to learn how to draw Mickey and Minnie Mouse. It's easy and lots of fun. So gather your art supplies and let's begin!

YOU'LL NEED A PENCIL.
(NUMBER 2 IS BEST.)

USE AN ERASER TO ERASE YOUR CONSTRUCTION PENCIL LINES AND MISTAKES.

BE SURE YOU HAVE A PENCIL SHARPENER, TO KEEP YOUR PENCILS SHARP.

YOU'LL NEED SOME PLAIN PAPER FOR PRACTICE. A SKETCH PAD WOULD BE BEST!

COLLECT A BLACK FELT-TIP PEN AND AS MANY COLORED PENCILS AS YOU CAN FIND.

NOW THAT YOU HAVE EVERYTHING, TURN THE PAGE AND LET THE FUN BEGIN!

Getting the Right Shape

Practice drawing some different lines and shapes that will help you to draw Mickey and Minnie. Draw light lines over light lines until you get the right shape.

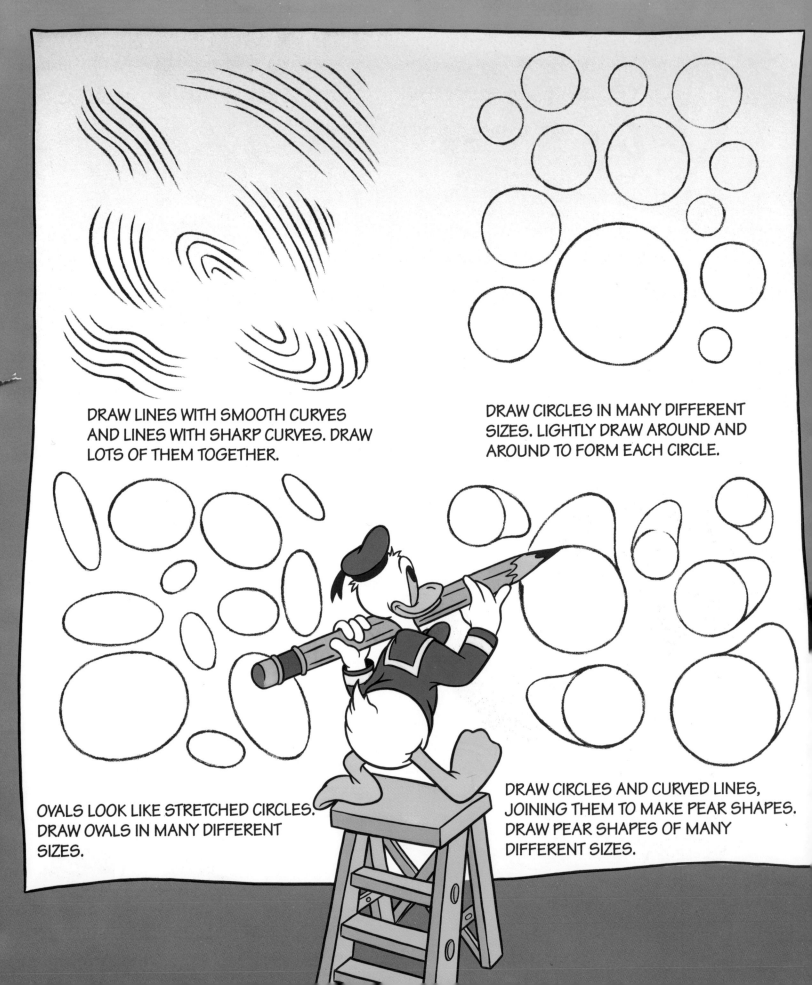

DRAW LINES WITH SMOOTH CURVES AND LINES WITH SHARP CURVES. DRAW LOTS OF THEM TOGETHER.

DRAW CIRCLES IN MANY DIFFERENT SIZES. LIGHTLY DRAW AROUND AND AROUND TO FORM EACH CIRCLE.

OVALS LOOK LIKE STRETCHED CIRCLES. DRAW OVALS IN MANY DIFFERENT SIZES.

DRAW CIRCLES AND CURVED LINES, JOINING THEM TO MAKE PEAR SHAPES. DRAW PEAR SHAPES OF MANY DIFFERENT SIZES.

Finishing Off

Let's see how Donald, Mickey, and Minnie turn a pencil sketch into a finished drawing.

DONALD DRAWS MICKEY'S HEAD IN PENCIL, DRAWING LIGHTLY UNTIL HE HAS ALL THE RIGHT SHAPES.

MICKEY CAREFULLY ERASES THE PENCIL LINES THAT ARE NOT NEEDED.

MINNIE USES A BLACK FELT-TIP PEN TO OUTLINE THE PENCIL DRAWING. WHEN THE INK DRIES, SHE'LL ERASE THE STRAY PENCIL LINES AND COLOR MICKEY'S FACE!

Let's Draw Mickey's Head

You can draw Mickey's head with just a few circles, ovals, and curved lines. The blue lines show you each new step of the drawing you should make.

1 LIGHTLY DRAW A CIRCLE. ADD CENTER LINES. THESE WILL HELP YOU TO POSITION MICKEY'S FEATURES.

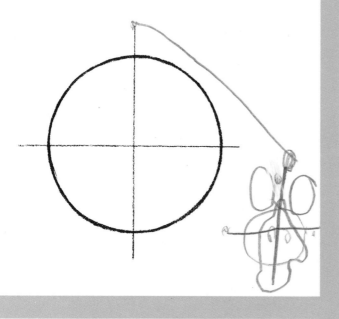

2 DRAW OVALS, LIKE SLIGHTLY STRETCHED CIRCLES, TO MAKE MICKEY'S EARS. THE OVALS SHOULD JUST TOUCH THE CIRCLE YOU HAVE DRAWN.

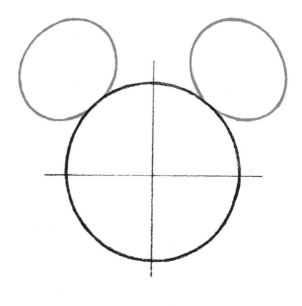

5 DRAW A CURVED LINE UNDER THE EYES TO MAKE MICKEY'S MUZZLE. THIS LINE SHOULD JUST TOUCH MICKEY'S EYES. ADD AN OVAL FOR HIS NOSE, AND ANOTHER OVAL TO HIGHLIGHT HIS NOSE.

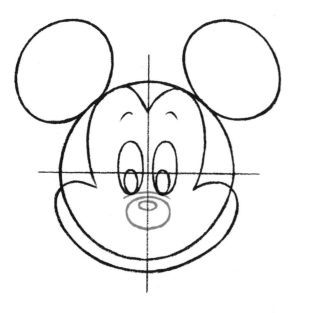

6 DRAW A CURVED LINE TO MAKE MICKEY SMILE AND TWO MORE CURVES TO FORM HIS MOUTH AND LOWER LIP. ADD THE TONGUE. NOTE THAT THE BOTTOM OF MICKEY'S MOUTH OVERLAPS THE CURVED CHEEKLINE YOU HAVE DRAWN.

Remember to draw each step lightly. If you make a mistake, use your eraser to gently remove the unwanted lines.

3 DRAW CURVED LINES TO FORM THE CHEEKS AND THE SHAPE AROUND MICKEY'S EYES (THE "EYE MASK" AREA). NOTE THAT THE CHEEKS ARE WIDER AND LOWER THAN THE CIRCLE.

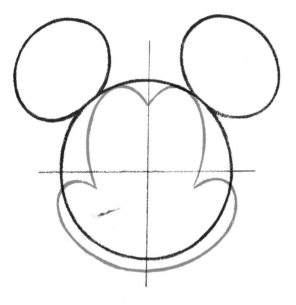

4 DRAW THIN OVALS, WITH SMALLER OVALS INSIDE, FOR MICKEY'S EYES AND PUPILS. ADD CURVES FOR THE EYEBROWS.

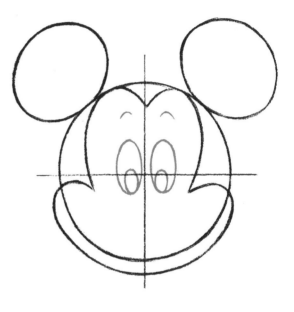

7 GENTLY ERASE THE CONSTRUCTION LINES AND CLEAN UP THE DRAWING.

8 NOW CAREFULLY OUTLINE YOUR DRAWING WITH A BLACK FELT-TIP PEN. WHEN THE INK DRIES, ERASE ANY STRAY PENCIL LINES AND COLOR IN MICKEY!

Let's Draw Minnie's Head

Use circles, ovals, and curved lines to draw Minnie's head too. Minnie and Mickey are similar, but look out for some details that are different.

1 LIGHTLY DRAW A CIRCLE. ADD CENTER LINES.

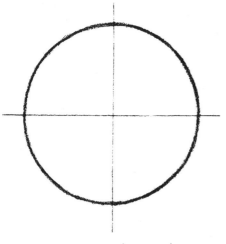

2 DRAW OVALS, LIKE SLIGHTLY STRETCHED CIRCLES, TO MAKE MINNIE'S EARS. THESE OVALS SHOULD BARELY TOUCH THE CIRCLE YOU HAVE DRAWN.

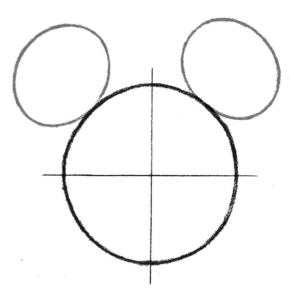

5 DRAW A CURVED LINE JUST TOUCHING THE EYES TO MAKE MINNIE'S MUZZLE. DRAW AN OVAL SHAPE FOR HER NOSE AND A SMALLER OVAL INSIDE TO HIGHLIGHT HER NOSE.

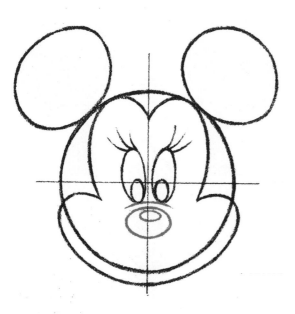

6 DRAW CURVES TO FORM MINNIE'S MOUTH, LOWER LIP, AND SMILE. ADD HER TONGUE AND THE CURVED LINES THAT FORM HER BOW.

Remember to draw lightly and use your eraser to remove stray pencil lines as you draw each new step shown in blue.

 3 DRAW CURVED LINES TO FORM MINNIE'S CHEEKS AND THE EYE MASK AREA (THE SHAPE AROUND MINNIE'S EYES).

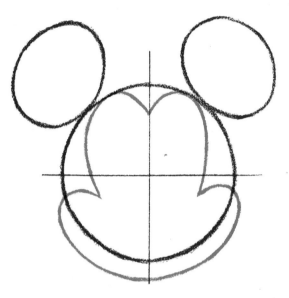

4 DRAW OVALS FOR MINNIE'S EYES. DRAW SMALLER OVALS INSIDE FOR THE PUPILS. ADD THREE CURVED LINES FOR THE EYELASHES.

 7 ERASE THE UNWANTED PENCIL LINES AND CLEAN UP THE DRAWING.

 8 USE A BLACK FELT-TIP PEN TO OUTLINE YOUR DRAWING. COLOR IN MINNIE ONCE THE INK HAS DRIED, AND YOUR MINNIE FACE IS NOW COMPLETE!

The 3/4 View — Mickey

The most popular view of Mickey is the 3/4 view. This view is not directly from the front nor directly from the side. In this drawing, Mickey will be looking to the right.

1 START WITH A CIRCLE. ADD TWO CENTER LINES. IN THE 3/4 VIEW, THESE CENTER LINES SHOULD CURVE, WRAPPING AROUND THE CIRCLE. SINCE MICKEY IS GOING TO BE LOOKING TO THE RIGHT, THE VERTICAL CENTER LINE CURVES IN THE DIRECTION HE IS LOOKING.

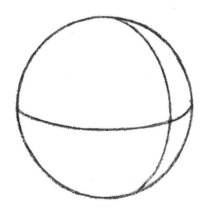

2 TO DRAW MICKEY'S EARS, ADD TWO OVALS: ONE AT THE TOP OF THE CIRCLE, AND ONE AT THE SIDE.

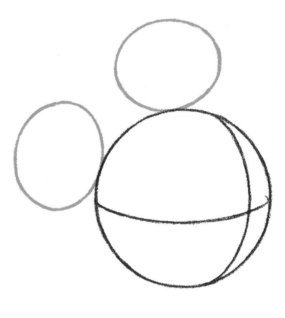

5 TO MAKE MICKEY'S MUZZLE AND MOUTH, DRAW A CURVED LINE, STARTING JUST BELOW THE EYES AND ENDING IN THE CHEEK AREA. ADD OVALS FOR MICKEY'S NOSE AND HIGHLIGHT.

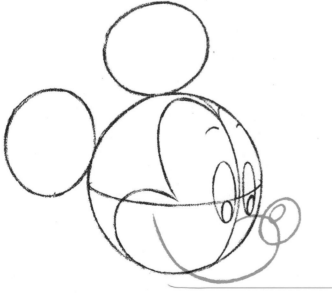

6 DRAW CURVED LINES TO MAKE MICKEY'S MOUTH, TONGUE, AND LOWER LIP. NOTICE HOW THE LOWER LIP DROPS BELOW THE BIG CIRCLE.

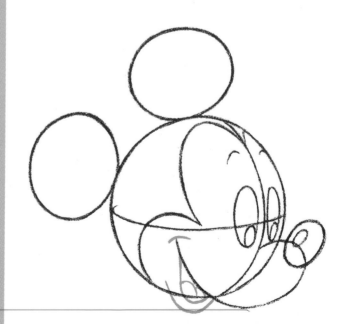

3 NOW DRAW THREE CURVED LINES TO MAKE MICKEY'S CHEEK AND EYE MASK AREA. NOTICE WHERE THESE CURVES HIT THE CENTER LINES AND THE BOTTOM OF THE CIRCLE.

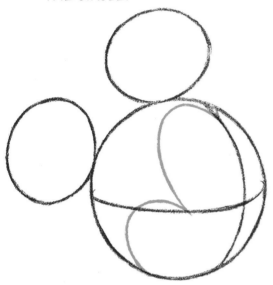

4 DRAW THIN OVALS FOR MICKEY'S EYES ON EITHER SIDE OF THE VERTICAL CENTER LINE. ADD TWO SMALLER OVALS FOR THE PUPILS, AND TWO CURVES FOR THE EYEBROWS.

7 GENTLY ERASE THE CONSTRUCTION LINES.

8 USE YOUR FELT-TIP PEN TO OUTLINE THE DRAWING. NOW YOU CAN ERASE ANY STRAY PENCIL LINES — AND COLOR IN MICKEY!

The 3/4 View — Minnie

1 LIGHTLY DRAW A CIRCLE. DRAW TWO CURVED CENTER LINES, ONE THAT WRAPS AROUND THE CIRCLE TOP TO BOTTOM, THE OTHER, SIDE TO SIDE.

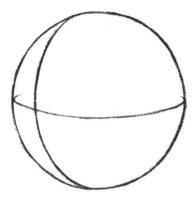

2 NEXT, ADD ONE OVAL TO THE TOP OF THE CIRCLE AND ANOTHER TO THE RIGHT SIDE. YOU'VE JUST DRAWN MINNIE'S EARS!

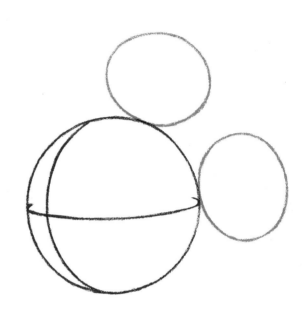

5 MINNIE'S MUZZLE IS ONE LONG CURVED LINE STARTING JUST BELOW HER EYES AND ENDING IN HER CHEEK AREA. DRAW A SMALL OVAL ON THE END OF THE MUZZLE TO GIVE MINNIE A NOSE. ADD THE OVAL HIGHLIGHT.

6 DRAW MINNIE'S MOUTH WITH A CURVED LINE ATTACHED TO THE MUZZLE. ADD MORE CURVED LINES AND YOU'VE DRAWN MINNIE'S TONGUE AND LOWER LIP! USE CURVED LINES FOR MINNIE'S BOW.

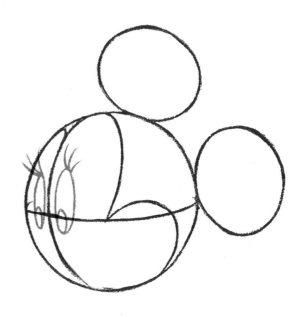

3 TO FORM MINNIE'S EYE MASK AREA AND CHEEK, DRAW THREE CURVED LINES. THE LOWEST CURVE IS THE FATTEST, THE MIDDLE IS THE TALLEST, AND THE LAST ONE IS SMALLEST AND MOST NARROW.

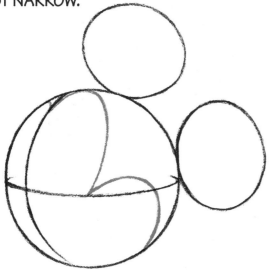

4 DRAW MINNIE'S EYES AND PUPILS WITH TWO SMALL OVALS INSIDE TWO LARGER ONES. THE EYES GO ON EITHER SIDE OF THE VERTICAL CENTER LINE.

7 CAREFULLY ERASE THE UNWANTED LINES.

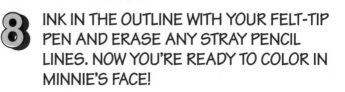

8 INK IN THE OUTLINE WITH YOUR FELT-TIP PEN AND ERASE ANY STRAY PENCIL LINES. NOW YOU'RE READY TO COLOR IN MINNIE'S FACE!

Mickey's Expressions

Mickey's facial features are very flexible. They squash and stretch to help him express his different attitudes and moods. Notice how the mouth, cheeks, eyes, and mask area change to form these expressions.

MICKEY LOOKS ANGRY WHEN YOU BRING THE CENTER OF THE MASK AREA DOWN OVER THE EYES, REMOVE HIS EYEBROWS, LOWER THE CHEEKS, AND CURVE DOWN THE MOUTH.

HIGH CHEEKS AND A BIG, OPEN-MOUTHED SMILE MAKE A HAPPY MICKEY.

CURVE DOWN THE EYE MASK, SLOPE THE EYES AND EYEBROWS, LOWER THE CHEEK LINE, AND TURN DOWN THE MOUTH TO MAKE MICKEY LOOK SAD OR WORRIED.

TO MAKE MICKEY LOOK SURPRISED, STRETCH HIS WHOLE HEAD, HIS EYES, AND HIS EARS.

Let's Draw Hands

You'll notice Mickey and Minnie always wear gloves. Their hands are round, with three sausage-like fingers and a thumb. Try steps 1-4 and you'll get the idea!

1 DRAW A CIRCLE FOR THE PALM OF THE HAND. NOW ADD A CURVED LINE GOING FROM ONE SIDE OF THE CIRCLE TO THE OTHER, CREATING A LONG PEAR SHAPE. OPPOSITE THIS CURVE, DRAW TWO LINES FOR THE ARM.

2 THE THUMB IS A STUBBY SAUSAGE SHAPE WITH A WIDE, CURVED BASE. THIS BASE STARTS AT THE ARM ON ONE SIDE OF THE PALM, AND ENDS AT THE FINGERS.

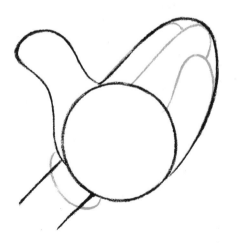

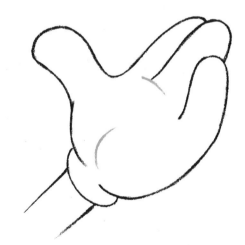

3 DRAW THREE LONG SAUSAGE SHAPES FOR THE FINGERS. DON'T LET THE BASE OF THE FINGERS DROP INSIDE THE CIRCLE. ADD A CUFF TO THE GLOVE.

4 DRAW A CURVED PALM LINE. NOW ERASE THE UNWANTED LINES.

Mickey Standing

Mickey is three heads tall. This means that if you draw three circles the size of Mickey's head, one on top of the other, that is how tall Mickey should be.

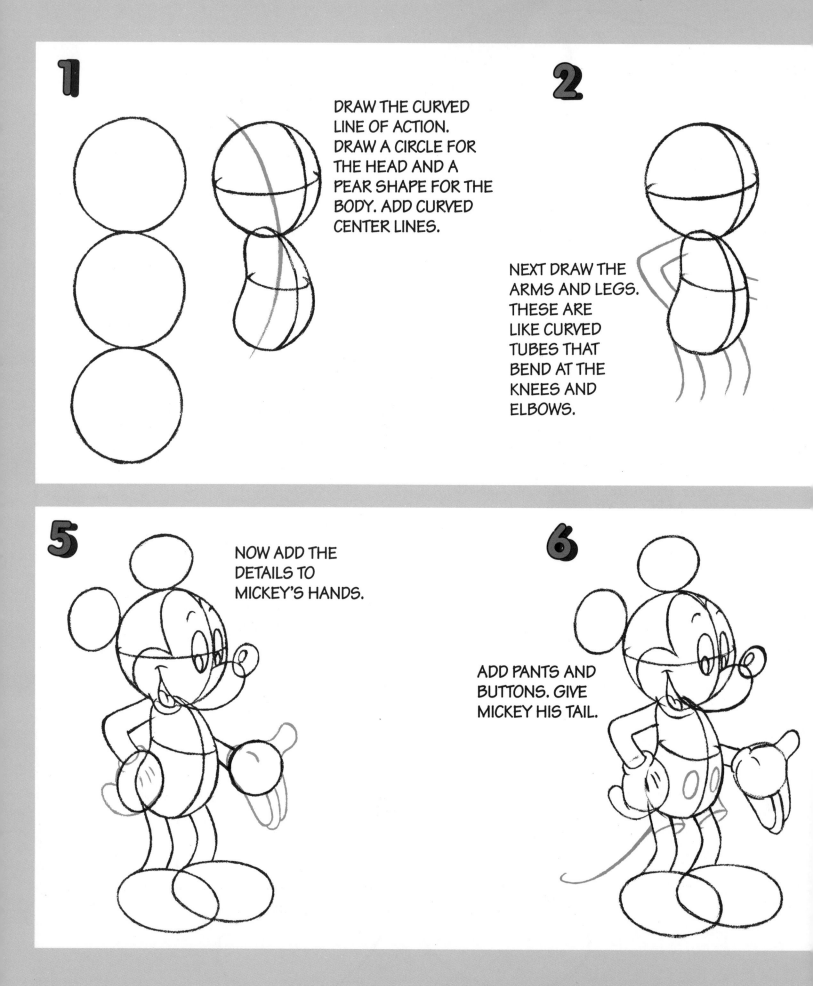

1

DRAW THE CURVED LINE OF ACTION. DRAW A CIRCLE FOR THE HEAD AND A PEAR SHAPE FOR THE BODY. ADD CURVED CENTER LINES.

2

NEXT DRAW THE ARMS AND LEGS. THESE ARE LIKE CURVED TUBES THAT BEND AT THE KNEES AND ELBOWS.

5

NOW ADD THE DETAILS TO MICKEY'S HANDS.

6

ADD PANTS AND BUTTONS. GIVE MICKEY HIS TAIL.

When you draw Mickey standing, start by drawing a line of action. The line of action is a guideline to help you give your character direction and movement.

3

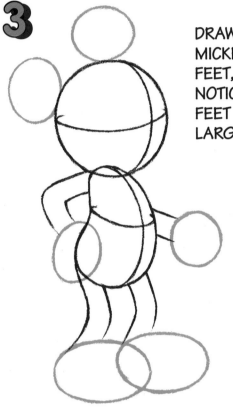

DRAW OVALS FOR MICKEY'S HANDS, FEET, AND EARS. NOTICE THAT THE FEET ARE THE LARGEST OVALS.

4

ADD THE FEATURES ON MICKEY'S FACE AS YOU LEARNED TO DO BEFORE. ALWAYS GIVE MICKEY A LIVELY EXPRESSION.

7

DRAW MICKEY'S SHOES, AND THEN GENTLY ERASE THE CONSTRUCTION LINES.

8

USE YOUR PEN TO INK IN THE DRAWING. ERASE ANY STRAY PENCIL LINES. NOW YOU'RE READY TO COLOR!

Minnie Standing

Minnie is three heads tall. That means that if you stack three balls the size of Minnie's head, one on top of the other, that is how tall Minnie should be.

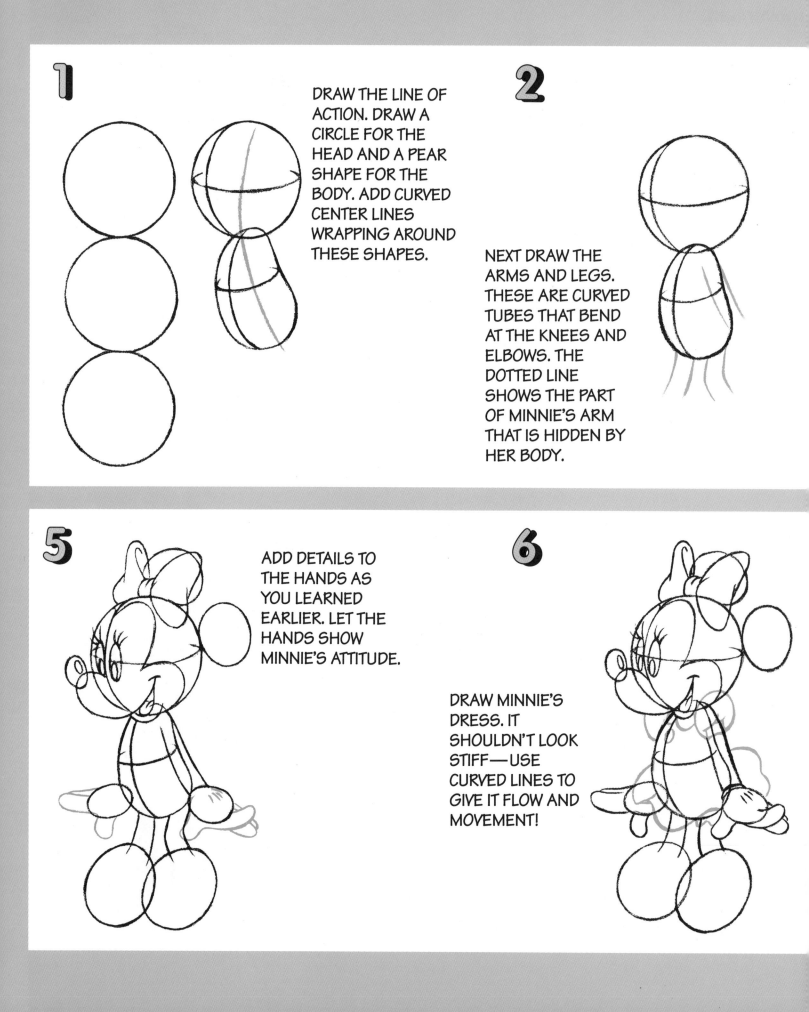

1

DRAW THE LINE OF ACTION. DRAW A CIRCLE FOR THE HEAD AND A PEAR SHAPE FOR THE BODY. ADD CURVED CENTER LINES WRAPPING AROUND THESE SHAPES.

2

NEXT DRAW THE ARMS AND LEGS. THESE ARE CURVED TUBES THAT BEND AT THE KNEES AND ELBOWS. THE DOTTED LINE SHOWS THE PART OF MINNIE'S ARM THAT IS HIDDEN BY HER BODY.

5

ADD DETAILS TO THE HANDS AS YOU LEARNED EARLIER. LET THE HANDS SHOW MINNIE'S ATTITUDE.

6

DRAW MINNIE'S DRESS. IT SHOULDN'T LOOK STIFF—USE CURVED LINES TO GIVE IT FLOW AND MOVEMENT!

When drawing a standing Minnie, begin by drawing a line of action. The line of action is a guideline that helps you give your character direction and movement.

3

DRAW OVALS FOR THE HANDS, EARS, AND FEET. MAKE SURE THAT YOU DRAW LARGER OVALS FOR THE FEET.

4

ADD THE FACIAL FEATURES AND THE BOW ON MINNIE'S HEAD.

7

ADD MINNIE'S SHOES AND TAIL, AND ERASE UNWANTED PENCIL LINES. NOTICE HOW EVEN HER FEET ARE EXPRESSIVE!

8

NOW YOU'RE READY TO INK IN THE OUTLINE AND COLOR IN MINNIE!

More Hands

MICKEY'S AND MINNIE'S HANDS HAVE THREE SHORT LINES ON THE BACK. THESE LINES FOLLOW THE ROUND SHAPE OF THE GLOVE.

AFTER YOU'VE DRAWN THESE HANDS, TRY SOME OF YOUR OWN. WITH A LITTLE PRACTICE, YOU'LL BE A PRO, JUST LIKE GOOFY.

Minnie's Expressions

Notice how flexible Minnie's chin, cheeks, and mouth are. Her eye mask and eyes also stretch, squash, and change position, all reflecting different expressions.

YOU CAN CREATE A *CURIOUS* MINNIE USING WIDE-OPEN EYES AND A SMALL OVAL MOUTH.

MINNIE'S MASK AREA SLOPES IN ABOVE HER EYES WHEN SHE IS *SHY* OR *EMBARRASSED*.

TO MAKE MINNIE LOOK *ALOOF* OR *DISINTERESTED*, CLOSE HER EYES, LOWER THE CURVE OF HER CHEEK, AND TURN DOWN HER MOUTH.

HIGH CHEEKS AND A BIG, OPEN-MOUTHED SMILE MAKE A VERY *JOYFUL* MINNIE!

Minnie Walking
Mickey Running

When you want to draw Mickey or Minnie in action, it's often helpful to look in a mirror to see how you yourself would move. You can also *imagine* yourself walking or running.

1

LIGHTLY DRAW THE LINE OF ACTION, A CIRCLE WITH CURVED CENTER LINES FOR THE HEAD, AND A PEAR SHAPE WITH CURVED CENTER LINES FOR THE BODY. ADD CURVED TUBES FOR ARMS AND LEGS AND OVALS FOR EARS, HANDS, AND FEET.

2

FILL IN THE DETAILS OF MINNIE'S FACE, HANDS, SHOES, AND TAIL, USING OVALS AND CURVED LINES.

1

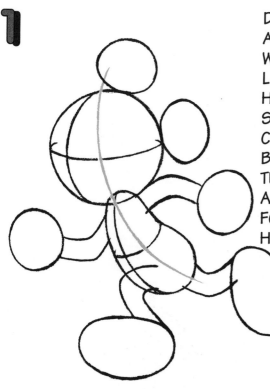

DRAW THE LINE OF ACTION, A CIRCLE WITH CURVED CENTER LINES FOR MICKEY'S HEAD AND A PEAR SHAPE WITH CURVED CENTER LINES FOR HIS BODY. ADD CURVED TUBES FOR HIS ARMS AND LEGS AND OVALS FOR HIS EARS, HANDS, AND FEET.

2

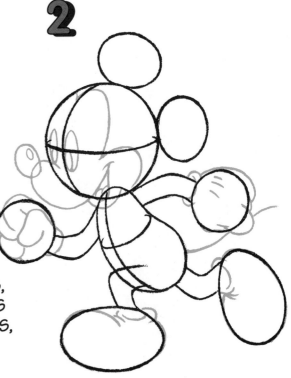

USING CURVED LINES AND OVALS, DRAW IN MICKEY'S FACE, TAIL, GLOVES, AND SHOES.

But always be sure to give your drawings extra zip and movement. Now try to capture and exaggerate that feeling as you follow these steps.

3

ADD MINNIE'S BOW AND DRESS, AS YOU'VE LEARNED ON THE PREVIOUS PAGES. LET HER SKIRT SWING AS SHE MOVES.

4

GENTLY ERASE THE UNWANTED PENCIL LINES. NOW YOU'RE READY TO INK AND COLOR IN MINNIE!

3

DRESS MICKEY FOR A REAL WORKOUT. ADD A SWEAT BAND, A TANK TOP, AND SHORTS.

4

CLEAN UP THE DRAWING, AND INK AND COLOR IN MICKEY!

Action Poses

MICKEY LOVES EVERY SPORT YOU CAN THINK OF! REMEMBER, ALWAYS START WITH THE LINE OF ACTION TO GET A STRONG SENSE OF MOVEMENT. AFTER YOU'VE PRACTICED THESE POSES, TRY SOME OF YOUR OWN. HOW ABOUT SWIMMING, TENNIS, OR SKIPPING ROPE?

IT'S EASY TO GUESS SOME OF MINNIE'S FAVORITE PASTIMES! DANCING, PICKING FLOWERS, AND ROLLER-SKATING ARE ONLY THREE OF THE THINGS MINNIE ENJOYS. WHAT OTHER ACTIVITIES CAN YOU DRAW? GIVE ALL OF YOUR DRAWINGS THAT "MINNIE" FEELING!

Coloring Tips

So far, you've been filling in your drawings with flat areas of solid tone or color. There are many other ways of finishing your pictures once you're done drawing the characters. Here are just a few ideas.

DONALD AND MICKEY ARE GIVING MINNIE A SOFT, ROUNDED LOOK BY GENTLY SHADING THE LOWER PART OF HER MUZZLE AND CHIN. THEY GIVE THE SAME FEEL TO HER BOW.

MINNIE'S REALLY SETTING MICKEY'S FEET ON THE GROUND BY ADDING SOME WISPY BLADES OF GRASS AROUND AND IN FRONT OF HIS FEET.

Other Ways to Color

Pencil and felt-tip pen are only two of the many materials you can choose to create your finished drawings. Here are some other possibilities.

DONALD USES WATERCOLORS AND A PAINT BRUSH TO BRING MICKEY TO LIFE!

GOOFY PUTS HIS BEST FOOT FORWARD USING POSTER PAINTS.

BE LIKE MICKEY, AND GIVE MINNIE A BRIGHT COMPLEXION WITH COLORED MARKERS!